MUSINGS
Delightful Stories from a Long Life

James H. Hardy

MUSINGS
Delightful Stories from a Long Life

Copyright, 2018
James H. Hardy

All rights reserved
First Edition, 2018

Cover layout and interior pages
layout by Capri Porter.

Printed in the United States of America

ISBN: 978-1-7322135-2-4

Published by Legacies & Memories
St. Augustine, Florida

(888) 862-2754
www.LegaciesandMemories.com

Contents

Preface
Grammie...9
Sour Milk...15
Father...21
Herman...27
Railroading...33
Expulsion...39
Mister Balsley...43
Biology...47
The Lampoon...51
"No-Squeak" Lee...55
Christmas Tree...59
The Pigs...63
The Fall of Mary...67
The Raccoon...73
Overseas Adventure 1...77
Overseas Adventure 2...81
Overseas Adventure 3...85

Mako Shark...89
First Solo...95
Ebony...99
Physical Therapy...105
Bad Timing...107
Canoe Club Cannon...111
The Pill...115
Trees...119
Draft Horse...125
George...129
Gardening...131
What to Do...135
The Circle...139
Acknowledgments...143
About the Author...145

Preface

Whether writing about family members such as Grammie or Grandfather Rapp, or about topics as varied as overseas travel, the U.S. Navy, trees, a baby raccoon, raising pigs as part of a 4-H project, the *Harvard Lampoon*, sour milk, or a Mako Shark, James H. Hardy's thirty stories in this collection are a delight to read. Fun and amusing are fitting descriptions.

He enjoys a good story, and although he claims to write partly because of boredom, the truth is that he has long been motivated to chronicle the interesting, humorous and poignant moments of life from childhood to today. He previously penned sixty-five stories in a collection that was published in 2016.

As a retired orthopedic surgeon following forty years in medicine, he has time to reminisce and reflect on interesting incidents, events and stories that happened to him or others. Life is full of such moments, especially a life spanning more than eight decades. His musings are a joy to read.

– *Publisher, Legacies & Memories*

MUSINGS
Delightful Stories from a Long Life

GRAMMIE

My father's mother, Grammie, played a significant role in our life. She was born into a 19th-century immigrant household on North 13th Street in Philadelphia, a densely populated Irish Catholic enclave that turned out powerful and successful politicians and businessmen. The area was also home to the Kelly family of rowing and Monaco fame, the "Big Daddy" Flanigan food purveyors and spirits distributors, and the Dougherty distillery that produced excellent red-label rye whiskey and a premium black-label whiskey before Prohibition went into effect.

Grammie was one of six or seven or eight kids. Her father, my great-grandfather, was the Philadelphia parks commissioner, overseeing Fairmount Park and its environs – at the time, the largest urban open space in the world. We loved her tales of trips to Woodside Amusement Park on the open trolley, a classic entertainment of that period.

Grammie graduated from Normal School and planned to teach school at the turn of the century, but instead married Jim Hardy, a charismatic Protestant boy from rural Massachusetts. After finishing Exeter in the class of 1898, he studied at the University of Pennsylvania Medical School.

My father was born in 1903. After about four years, Grammie and Grandfather Hardy divorced and both independently drifted to New York City.

Grammie worked for Park & Tilford, an upscale department store that went belly-up in the 1930s during the Great Depression. When her employment ended, she negotiated a deal with the director of the cosmetics division to buy his patents and formula book. These she used to produce the Marie Hervey brand of cosmetics, thus supporting herself and her sister Ruth for several years.

Grammie lived with her sister, Ruth, a militant who was probably partially responsible for the breakup of her sister's marriage.

Ruth developed her own business as a seamstress, making beautiful dresses in a small area of their one-room apartment that she partitioned off with a floor-to-ceiling piece of fiberboard. She was very good at what she did, counting among her customers such luminaries as opera singer Lily Pons and actress Deanna Durbin.

Times were tough for these ladies – federal assistance didn't exist then. Grammie walked to and from work at the Essex House, located at Sixth Avenue and Central Park South (59th Street), every day, including Saturday. There she gave treatments and demonstrated and sold her goods. Believe it or not, she personally made all her products in the cramped little kitchen of their apartment.

My first recollection of visiting Grammie in New York – I believe they lived on West 84th Street at the time – was going to the end of the street and hanging over a railing in the dark to watch a chugging ancient diesel engine pushing freight cars around in the yard below.

Subsequently Grammie and Aunt Ruth lived at 307 E. 57th Street. Aunt Ruth loved birds and had built several nesting areas in their ground-floor apartment as well as a bird cage outside that protruded over the sidewalk and housed a score of canaries. As the birds sang cheerily away, people on the sidewalk would stop and stare, totally charmed.

One of the fun highlights of each year was watching the "elephant walk" from the windows of Grammie's place on 57th Street when the circus came to town to perform at the famed Madison Square Garden.

The routine for decades was to park the circus train in Jamaica Yard on Long Island and then parade some of the animals on foot and the rest in cages on wagons. The route took them over the 59th Street bridge and on to Madison Square Garden via 57th Street.

We barely dozed as we eagerly awaited the grand procession held late at night to avoid crowds and traffic. Amazingly, most of the excited sounds we heard came from ourselves as the animals – elephants, horses, camels, lions, and tigers in rolling cages – quietly passed by our windows.

Eventually the circus no longer arrived at

the Jamaica Yard, and the era of the midnight circus parade died. Ultimately so did everyone else. Aunt Ruth died of heart failure at Bellevue Hospital in New York City. Grammie died while living with my parents. The building that had housed their apartment and their charming canaries was demolished.

307 E. 57th St. may have been erased from the face of Manhattan, but it lives vividly in my memories.

No one else may remember 307 E. 57th St., but I know the elephants remember the midnight parades – and I remember the elephants!

SOUR MILK

Our summer abode, one of Grandfather Rapp's rental properties, was in Ocean City, New Jersey, where we joined scores of other Philadelphians as well as multitudes of cousins and other relatives. Because my mother helped get the rental ready each summer, we could stay there until the renters arrived. We all enjoyed the sea breeze and the short walk to the beach.

On one side of the rental was a large vacant lot with a massive sand pit that became our personal sandbox. We spent many happy hours there imagining splendid adventures as we played with our toy soldiers and trucks.

The high point of the day was my father's arrival on the commuter train from Philadelphia. We could hear the steam whistle when the train reached Tenth Street, which gave us just enough time to scamper up the street to The Gardens Station, the end of line, to meet it. The steam engine just sat there, but it was alive and breathing, with a pulse and a special warmth radiating from it. Leaning out of the engineer's window was Walter – I never learned his last name, but he was my all-time hero. On a couple occasions, after the engine was turned around on the "Y," he let me sit on his lap as it returned to the overnight and servicing area. There was no greater thrill for a boy of 6 ... or 7 ... or 8.

The next order of business was to walk home with father, change into our bathing suits, and skip down to the beach for a late afternoon dip. Then a cold outdoor shower, a change of clothes, and we were ready for dinner.

"Oh dear, we're out of milk!" cried mother. "Jimmy, would you please hop across the street to Freida's Deli and get a quart of milk? Here's some change."

Spurred on by mounting hunger, I trotted across the street and opened the screen door to the ground-floor store. The door tinkled as it closed, and down from upstairs lumbered Mr. "Freida," the man of the house – a gruff, rotund, mustachioed gentleman never known to smile or laugh in public.

"One quart of milk, please."

"Okay, sonny, here you are," he said, while reaching into the large cooler behind the counter.

I gave him the money and headed home. Everyone was happily seated around the kitchen table waiting for me. Mother opened the milk, made a terrible face, and exclaimed, "It's sour! Here, Jimmy, please return this and get a fresh one."

So, out the door, across the street, through the tinkling screen door. Again, down came Freida's husband, even less convivial than before.

"Whaddya want now?" he growled.

"This milk I just got was sour and my folks sent me to get a new one."

"What?!" shouted the man with the big mustache, "you must have swapped it at home. Get out of here!"

Back home I trudged. Father listened to my story, gradually getting angrier than I had ever seen him. "Come on, son, we'll take the milk back," he said.

We marched out the door, father walking so

fast and forcefully that I had to hop and skip to keep up, even though I had ahold of his little finger. He was snapping his fingers loudly and rapidly. Into the shop we went. No tinkle-tinkle this time, but bang – clang – clang!

Freida's husband must have had a premonition that all was not well, because he looked very defensive, standing behind the counter on the left side of the shop in front of shelves of Campbell's soup.

"Whaddya want?" he said, while easing back toward the soup cans.

Father said, "Here's your sour milk. I would like a fresh one."

Mr. Mustache growled something like "Rotten kid!"

Father lunged toward the counter. The mustache reached back for a soup can.

Father hissed between clenched teeth, "Put that down, now! Get me one bottle of milk." I could see the muscles around his jaw twitching.

The mustache man obviously reconsidered his hostile behavior. He sullenly reached into his cooler, thrust a new quart of milk at father, and snarled, "Now get out of my store."

That we did quite promptly!

That was about seventy-five years ago, and I believe I'm the only surviving witness to the battle of Ocean Avenue. I can assure you that no one in our large extended family ever went near Freida's Deli again!

FATHER

My father, a Philadelphia lawyer who spoke carefully and correctly, also had the ability to make the English language enjoyable and almost delightful. One early example was his description of a football practice at Columbia University in which he competed with future baseball legend Lou Gehrig for a position on the team, despite Gehrig being a couple years his senior. They had been matched through the fate of the alphabet, with Hardy following Gehrig. They lined up for tackling drills – coach Percy Haughton blew his whistle – and mayhem ensued as the two players charged each other.

"Like trying to tackle an oak tree," father described it later. Thus, a phrase entered our family's vocabulary that had real meaning when facing an insoluble problem.

In the winter of his junior year, father

contracted pneumonia and was hospitalized, placed in the "Norrie 4" ward, where the cold room – actually, a screened porch – was used for the treatment of terminal pneumonia. Grammie told us he had received last rites and was just about gone. Somehow, he rallied, slowly recovered, and eventually returned to school. He spent that summer with relatives of his mother who had a place in Ocean City, New Jersey. The sun and fresh air were expected to rejuvenate him. They certainly did – he met the girl he later married, my mother.

Father entered Harvard Law School, so mother appropriately entered another Massachusetts school, Wheaton College, located in the city of Norton. Their visits with each other were conducted with some difficulty by public transportation – a trolley car – but it got the job done. On occasion the fond good-byes lasted a bit too long and the last car left without the lingering law student onboard. When this happened, father would race after the car and then grab the rope to the pole and pull it off the overhead electric wire – stopping everything, including the lighting. As the motorman got up and went out the front door on the right side, father would run up the left side, race around the front, and dart into a seat. Following father's graduation from law school in 1928, my parents were married in a blizzard in February 1929. I was born in November 1930. (My Grandfather and Grandmother Hardy were married in a blizzard in 1913. My wife and I were married in a blizzard in 1961. Nobody learned!)

Father practiced law with the firm of McCoy, Brittin, Evans, and Lewis. We lived in a small, semidetached house with a golf course on one side and a dairy farm behind. Father never swore or used the Lord's name in vain, having married into a Quaker family that had turned Episcopalian. Nevertheless, he seemed to have learned some satisfactory substitutes, most likely while working summers as a teenager, farming for his grandfather. Epithets such as "son of a sea cook!" and "drat!" seemed to suffice. This situation changed drastically after he returned from serving three years in the South Pacific during World War II, much to mother's horror. I, too, had developed some rather colorful expressions while serving a couple years in the Korean War, leading mother to exclaim on multiple occasions that the Navy had ruined her men!

As a lawyer, labor arbitrator and professor of law at Temple University, father considered precise wording to be of paramount importance in his professional – and home – life. As an important event was described in detail, he listened alertly – never dozing, never resting his eyes – until he had absorbed the entire explanation of the situation. Then, after a long, slow draw on his favorite pipe, he would lean back, exhale, and quietly say, "That's very interesting – if true." So much for that!

Father's life at Harvard Law School was also interesting. His roommate was Irwin Griswold, who later became dean of that very same school. Father's description of the dreaded final-exam process was frightening. Everything hinged on the final exams – pass or fail, sink or swim – a truly overwhelming experience. Father studied furiously for his finals, grilling himself day after day, late into the night, until exhausted – terrified of failing. All this time his roommate was spread out on the floor, working on his stamp collection!

Father served on the school board and took on Sunday school classes and other municipal projects. I remember after one particularly prickly school board meeting he exclaimed, "That woman has diarrhea of words with a constipation of ideas!" He went on to state, "I am not prejudiced, but I do have preferences."

After the war, father was there to guide, force unpleasant decisions and just plain support the operation. At one point, I was casting about for a college – a formidable task. Ultimately it boiled down to two choices: The University of Virginia accepted me with a full Navy ROTC scholarship, while Harvard also accepted me, but without financial aid or a scholarship. Total confusion reigned. I knew nothing of the family finances. I knew I had a younger sister coming along, and I knew father was sending funds to his mother and meeting myriad other demands, all on a 1940s faculty salary. Finally, I sat down with father, complete with his pipe and easy chair, and outlined my dilemma. Again, after appropriate attention to his pipe, he quietly said, "Fella, you'll never go wrong going to Harvard." That was it!

Years later I described a process father

applied to a matter now long forgotten. After lengthy discussion in fine detail, including my reasons for and against some plan of action, father sat stoically unmoved. Finally, exhaling and breaking his silence, he said, "Son, I do believe the wish is father of the thought."

Yes, yes it often is. Father, I miss you.

HERMAN

My father's cousin, Herman, was a delightful man about 20 years older than I. He grew up in Chevy Chase, Maryland, and attended the University of Maryland, where he distinguished himself on the baseball field.

My first real contact with him happened around 1935, when I was about four or five years old. My grandmother took me along on a Greyhound bus journey from Philadelphia to Washington, D.C. The interstate highway system was still in the future, so we traveled along old Route 1, the Baltimore Pike. My most remarkable memory of the trip was of another passenger buying me a Dixie Cup of ice cream at a rest stop.

We stayed with Grammie's younger sister, Mary, while Grammie worked on her cosmetics business. Herman was in and out of the house playing Minor League baseball. On several occasions he took the time to play with me in the large backyard, where an apple tree provided a generous supply of missiles for batting practice – unfortunately, there was also a generous supply of yellow jackets enjoying the sweet nectar of our missiles, ensuring an unhappy outcome.

Years later, Herman told me stories of his nomadic athletic career. As a pitcher for the University of Maryland team he was fondly nicknamed "Specs Medler" by the local sports writers because he had to wear glasses full time. He also played in the summer leagues, which he described as being composed in those days of "has-beens," "might-be's," and "hope-to-be's." Anyway, he played in the summer leagues to make money, a definite no-no if he wanted to keep his college eligibility. For this reason, Herman played under an assumed name and no one was the wiser. However, after one particularly impressive demonstration of hurling ability, he was surrounded by sports writers, one of whom said, "I see you wear glasses. The only other pitcher I ever saw wearing glasses was Specs Medler at Maryland. Do you know him?" Herman stopped dead, looked up at the sky, slowly shook his head, and said, "Do tell!" That was that.

After college he played some more ball, then pursued a job with the FBI, where his older brother held an influential position. Sadly, he was turned down when they discovered he had used an alias! What goes around comes around. He couldn't join the military either, due to his poor eyesight, but he finally landed a job driving a gasoline tank truck for Amoco Oil Company.

A couple years ago we visited Herman at the rehab facility where he was recovering from a heart-valve replacement. He had numerous yarns about semi-professional baseball that he was eager to share with us. Using the name "Dresser," he initially played in the Florida League, whose players had to travel to the ballpark on their own. If a game was posted, a player simply donned a uniform and presented himself to the local team manager. If chosen to join the team that day, a player would earn about twenty-five dollars – no tax withheld. Routinely the manager would ask, "What position do you play?" Herman's stock answer was, "You name it, I play it." Over time he played every position except catcher, but his favorite spot was pitcher. If no other pitcher showed up, Herman would pitch until the game was over. On a couple occasions he pitched both games of a doubleheader. He described that experience as pure torture – by the end of the second game his arm was so tired and sore that he could barely toss the ball to first base underhand.

The life of an itinerant ballplayer in the Depression years of the 1930s was a combination of frustration, desperation, and inspiration. Herman went on to describe for us many of his memorable fellow players from that era, especially those who were friends when he made the farm club for the Washington Senators. His favorite catcher was Jim "Iron Head" Galvin. Then there was a shortstop named Bobby Stevens who was an outstanding hitter and ultimately made it to the big leagues – but never got a hit off Herman, according to Herman! The umpire was usually a fellow named "Babe" Frome, who played on the defensive line of the Chicago Bears during the football season and umpired baseball in the summer to pick up some spending money. Apparently, his decisions were rarely disputed.

"Babe" Didrikson's younger brother was a frequent player. The manager was Bill "Rawmeat" Rodgers, whose son played with the team when they were in Sanford, Florida. His most distinguishing feature was that he had a bullet in his leg – no one knew the circumstances.

Herman loved playing baseball, talking baseball, and recollecting baseball. In later life, with his wife gone and his children scattered, he turned to ballroom dancing for diversion and entertainment. His dancing partners came and went until one partner just clicked. These events were the high point of his week, which otherwise revolved around his nursing home. I pressed for more details, and finally the facts emerged – his esteemed partner was none other than a retired Catholic nun! I told him I didn't know that nuns retired. I thought as long as they could swat a hand with a wooden ruler they were good to go. No, not true, Herman said.

We were getting ready to leave when Herman said, "I still talk with Bobby Stevens – he lives somewhere near Pittsburgh. You know, your idea about jotting down some of these stories is a good one."

We visited Herman in the summer of 2003 when he was ninety years old. "I guess we're about the last leaves on the tree," he said. I never got to talk to him again – he died that winter at age ninety-one.

RAILROADING

Two main routes led from home to my junior high school. The first, and most commonly used, was up our street, take a right on Manoa Road to the Haverford Township police station, and then left to Brookline and the school. The other route, used mostly in good weather, started off the same, but instead of turning on Manoa Road you continued to the end of that street, which came to a stop in a vacant field. Apparently World War II had canceled a plan to build houses there. Then across the field, through some scrub bushes, across an old, seldom-used railroad freight spur, into a group of houses, up a block, and there you were. Only rarely did local freight use the track. Larry and I had hitched a ride in an empty boxcar once and found ourselves at a farmer's market in Newtown Square when we got off, but that's another tale.

This latter route to school was shorter, but

much dirtier and completely devoid of interest. It was also so bumpy that if you rode your bike too fast you'd lose anything in your basket.

The semi-abandoned spur line was used by a local fuel company that had a small siding on a ramp that coal cars were pushed up to be loaded. A man from the coal company would open one of the hopper doors and deposit the coal into a waiting truck for delivery or into a pit for measuring and local resale. A significant number of the homes in this part of the country were heated by anthracite coal. This rail and truck arrangement brought the source and the consumer close together.

One evening on the way home from school my friends and I noticed a large, empty gondola car sitting all by itself on the ramp. It was full of scrap parts from the Autocar truck factory a couple miles away and was probably on its way to a scrapyard. Out of curiosity, we climbed aboard and started pawing through the junk. It was filthy, so I deposited my books on a clear place on the ground. We swarmed over the car like ants on a cookie. Someone got the smart idea to try to move the car. We saw a large, heavy metal and wooden pry bar lying on the ground and it didn't take long for us to figure out how to place it behind a wheel and get it moving. We realized this was the method workers probably used to adjust the placement of the car without a locomotive.

Given that we were on a slope, why not coast downhill? We released the brake by rotating the large wheel at the end of the car. Then one of us used the big pry bar to start the car rolling slowly down the hill. Very soon it was going too fast to jump off and no one was at the brake wheel. Fortunately, a derailer was fixed to the track to keep the car full of junk from moving onto the more traveled rails. Bang! We hit the derailer, which did its job perfectly. Then thump, thump, thump as the car bumped downward over the cross ties. Eventually it came to a quivering stop, we all got off, gathered our gear, and continued home.

It was several weeks before we spied another train car up on the delivery ramp. Our previous ride had been so much fun we decided to repeat. This time, though, I carefully put my Latin book and other papers over to the side, out of the way. I was riding the front of the rogue car and having fun when a loud voice shouted through a bullhorn, "Stand where you are – don't move!" A large policeman had appeared out of nowhere. Kids scattered like roaches when the light is turned on.

I realized I couldn't run because my books, with my name, address, class, and even my teacher's name, were on the ground, right where the policeman was standing. When defeat is inevitable, try to drag it out. So, I went up to the policeman and said, "Good afternoon, officer."

"Get in the car," was all he said.

I did so and discovered that the back seats of police cars don't have door handles. Off we went to the station. On the way, the policeman stopped and picked up my friend, Larry, on the other side of the woods. Obviously, the policeman had also gone to school here and was familiar with the geography of the area.

At the police station Larry and I were ushered into adjacent rooms, one staffed by the chief of police, the other by the head detective. After a half hour or so we swapped rooms and started all over again.

Finally, it was all over, and we were told to go home.

Outside, it was dark, late, and I still had a half-hour trudge ahead of me. Arriving home, I innocently marched in and said, "Hello." I had completely forgotten that my father had just come home on leave before deploying to the Pacific Theater during the war. A cold chill came over me, then a hot feeling of embarrassment, followed by the need to go to the bathroom. Oh, if only the bathroom had a back door!

"Where have you been?"

I gave the vaguest answer possible, followed by all sorts of excuses, alibis, and explanations – none of them any more factual than the story Larry and I had given the police.

After eating dinner alone and in silence, I went upstairs to do homework. It was apparent that my transgressions of the afternoon were not a major concern for the rest of the family. I could see that mother had been crying, so I figured it was not a good time to chat.

It was over a year and a half later when I next saw my father. He looked quite smart with battle ribbons on his chest as he disembarked the plane in his lieutenant-commander uniform. I waited patiently in line to greet him warmly. I was now older, in a different school – thanks in part to my uncles – and happy to let bygones be bygones.

EXPULSION

In the fall of 1947 our soccer team had become involved in a particularly contentious game with a local high school. Thinly veiled threats, and not so thinly veiled threats, were exchanged on the field out of earshot of the benches. Later in the game, verbal sparring morphed into physical actions that failed to attract interventions or warnings from the officials.

After becoming the unenviable recipient of two highly egregious but unnoticed episodes, I swore revenge. The ball was kicked toward the opposition goal. We dashed toward it full tilt. The offender, my nemesis, ran toward me. Without breaking stride, I cocked my fist, closed my eyes, and struck him as hard as I could, square in the face. I had never committed such a violent act in my life – truly I think it hurt me more than it did him.

That ended my participation for the day.

Back at school, I was summoned to the headmaster's office – a dark, ominous, oak paneled chamber, dominated by a large elephant-foot wastebasket.

"Hardy, what you did was ungentlemanly behavior," he said. "It will not be tolerated here. You are hereby dismissed from this school."

No discussion, no hearing, no excuses. I gathered my gear from the locker room, rode the bus to Sixty-Ninth Street, caught the trolley to Havertown, and walked dejectedly the last few blocks home.

"Hi," mother said. "How was your day?"

"Good."

"How did your team do?"

Embarrassingly, I realized that I didn't know who won the soccer game. I did know quite well that our record was less than stellar, so I made an educated guess and told her we had lost.

As was our routine, the next school day my father dropped me off on City Line across the street from my school on his way to Temple University, where he was a professor of law. I hopped out of the car and carefully crossed the street, but instead of entering my school I caught the next bus back to Sixty-Ninth Street. What I did the rest of that day is a complete blank.

The next day was the same routine, except I ducked into school to get the rest of my belongings.

"Oh, Hardy," Mr. Shinn called out from the shadows. "The headmaster wants to see you."

"Oh, great," I thought. "What more can he do to me now?"

"Come in, Hardy," the headmaster said. "I had a chat with your coach, Jimmy Mills, and he painted a different picture for me. [I have no idea who painted the first one.] I will cancel your expulsion and reinstate you as of now."

This was spectacular news – my life would return to normal.

To this day, my family has no inkling of what transpired that fateful afternoon at Episcopal Academy.

And I never did learn who won that awful game.

MISTER BALSLEY

I don't remember ever seeing Mr. Balsley break out in a whole-hearted laugh, but neither do I recall a grim frown or scowl, although Senior English in high school is a serious proposition. Not only can your teacher make or break your final year, but he's frequently involved in the college search and letters of recommendation. A demanding experience, but not totally without its lighter moments.

The Senior English class, attended by ten or twelve students at a boy's school in suburban Philadelphia founded in 1785, included intense concentration on S.I. Hayakawa's *Language in Thought and Action*. We discussed the finer points of grammar, the effective use of language, and other writing-related subjects. Our meeting place was the school's library, an appropriate venue, where shelves of silent, hidden knowledge waited to be discovered.

The furniture was stark – uncomfortable oak chairs and library tables.

Mr. Balsley possessed a distinctive appearance. He was rather short in stature, very lean, one might almost say cadaverous. His smooth, olive complexion was topped off by a shock of short-cropped, straight black hair, fringed with a sprinkling of gray.

He never sat down, just stood or paced slowly about the room while making a point. The rumor was that he ran great distances early in the morning, so naturally we assumed that he was continuing his cool-down with us, the first class of the day.

During discussions Mr. Balsley would propel his substantive but caustic comments with the skill of an archer, launching his perfectly directed darts straight into the heart of the topic. He despised "silly" talk and specious arguments and gave very few accolades. I never received one.

Most of the time my classmates and I were attentive. Nevertheless, there were some occasions when concentration and participation were less than maximal – and Mr. Balsley demanded maximal concentration.

As a case in point, one day in class, a buddy of mine, Dick Schneider, indicated he had something interesting to tell me. I made the mistake of leaning toward him across the table while Mr. Balsley was still talking, walking, and stalking. Suddenly, out of nowhere – Whomp! – a book slammed down on the top of my head. I was stunned not so much by the impact – *Language in Thought and Action* is a skinny tome – but by this unexpected assault. Without even a pause in his presentation, Mr. Balsley had gained my undivided attention.

Emotionally and physically I recovered from that unfortunate incident without a lawsuit or disability claim. The class concluded with the usual final requirements and exams, of which I have absolutely no recollection.

Registering for college, I learned that all freshmen were required to take English A, an introductory course. My group met at 1 p.m. on Monday afternoon – I have since been told by my progeny that no self-respecting college schedules a serious course after lunch these days.

My instructor, a graduate assistant, was very

smart, very eager, very earnestly working toward his advanced degree in English. As time went by, I started to notice him using certain words, phrases, and concepts that echoed Mr. Balsley's statements in Senior English. I thought for a while, then recalled that Mr. Balsley had taught in the highly esteemed Bread Loaf program at Middlebury College. Could there be a connection? Ultimately, it did turn out that my college instructor had attended Bread Loaf – so I received a double dose of knowledge! Mr. Balsley had mentored a student who in turn was mentoring me.

Nonetheless, College English was rather dull compared to Mr. Balsley's class, which was fascinating and even a little spicy.

You know what? I loved Mr. Balsley.

BIOLOGY

Encouraged by the hope of gaining local notoriety and the benefits that might accompany it, I offered to make a presentation featuring live snakes to my fellow classmates.

An acquaintance who worked for a local newspaper and happened to be an amateur herpetologist agreed to lend me his big indigo snake for my demonstration in biology class – Mr. Willing in charge.

This endeavor required borrowing the family car very early in the morning, traveling to Germantown – a suburb of Philadelphia that I thought required a special visa – fetching the snake, and then making it back to school in Merion in time for class at 9 a.m.

It sounds like a simple plan, but it was truly a tedious undertaking in morning traffic. First, I had to find Germantown. With that accomplished, I ended up in a neighborhood of identical brick rowhouses with white trim, all with white stone front steps and house numbers obscured by overgrown lilac bushes.

After a few embarrassing knocks at the wrong houses and glares from annoyed neighbors, I found the right place. The snake expert greeted me, then led me up a flight of stairs to the most magnificent male sanctuary I had ever seen.

Against the wall were cages containing many different animals and reptiles. The floor was crisscrossed by several model train tracks – the large variety with all sorts of scenery, tunnels, bridges, and decorations. The room's walls had been penetrated in several places to permit the trains to journey from room to room.

Suddenly, I realized that I needed to concentrate on the task at hand if I were to get to class on time.

The herpetologist proudly showed me his main pet, a large jet-black indigo snake. Wow! He told me he had fed her earlier that day because this species of constrictor does not have a lower jaw that dislocates to accommodate large prey, so it must eat small, frequent meals.

A beautiful leatherette carrying case was produced, padded with towels, snapped shut, and I was on my way.

The return trip was frustratingly slow due to traffic. Hearing the school bell ringing as I drove up, I figured I would slip in the back entrance to save time. It was a good idea but poorly executed, for there stood Mr. Shinn the disciplinarian filling out demerits. Oh well, a small price to pay to treat my classmates to a fascinating presentation!

I set the carrying case on the table at the front of the classroom and launched into my talk on reptiles, specifically indigo snakes. I pointed out that the indigo snake is nonvenomous, skilled at keeping vermin out of barns, and is honored as the state snake of Florida.

Detecting that my classmates' eyes were glazing over, I moved on to the presentation of the snake itself. I opened the case. To my shock, she was covered with slimy, sticky, white splotches – apparently having just excreted the remains of her morning meal. Fortunately, a sink and paper towels were nearby.

I began chattering about reptiles, snakes, and anything else that popped into my mind as I worked feverishly to clean up the mess. This part of the demonstration did appear to catch the attention of my audience – rather more attention than I desired.

Finally, I gathered up the snake to walk around the classroom, showing her off to various reactions of delight and disgust, brought the demonstration to an end, and sat down.

At the end of the day I retraced my steps to Germantown, returned the snake to her relieved owner, thanked him profusely, and left for home.

The snake's owner was not the only one quite relieved – of everything.

THE LAMPOON

Nothing appeared to delight members of the *Harvard Lampoon*, the university's humor publication, as much as tormenting figures of authority. Their targets sometimes included members of the college establishment, as well as strangers, but figures of authority were preferred. This latter group included politicians of all stripes, particularly those from nearby Boston.

One of my recollections is of a large formal reception with dinner, entertainment, and all the trimmings, meticulously staged and properly advertised. Formal dress required, naturally. The big night came, and guests started arriving. The crowd grew larger and larger until they realized it was all a big scam. This happened around the time of the Truman-Dewey presidential election, I believe.

In a similar affair, the *Lampoon* invited Massachusetts Governor Paul Dever to present a political lecture to the members. The governor agreed, and on the appointed evening arrived with a police motorcade escort. Being a person of rather generous proportions, he was carefully assisted from his chauffeured limo and up the steps into the lecture venue. As the honored guest entered, all the attendees politely rose from their tables – some 30-40 persons clad in pith helmets, dark glasses, Hawaiian shirts, loud shorts, and sandals – although it was midwinter! The governor gave a detailed, well-prepared speech, thanked the group profusely, and took his leave. Interesting evening!

On another memorable occasion, several *Lampoon* members slipped into the offices of the *Harvard Crimson*, the university's student newspaper, and made off with their ceremonial punch bowl. It was a large block of granite with the center hollowed out to form a bowl – and extremely heavy. To this day I can't understand how they managed to move it. Around the sides of the block was an engraved inscription, but I don't remember what it said, if I ever knew in the first place.

In the end, I never became a full *Lampoon*

member. I just didn't have the time, money, or dedication to make it possible. But I do have to give credit to the members – besides producing a quality humor magazine they also pulled off some hilarious stunts!

"NO-SQUEAK" LEE

Hong Kong! Macau! Intriguing and mystical Asian destinations. Usually after several months of shuttling back and forth from Japan to fuel the Seventh Fleet on the bombline in North Korea, a brief visit to Hong Kong for "R and R" was in order.

A large fleet oiler always drew a lot of attention on arrival, and almost immediately was surrounded by a plethora of "bum boats" bearing all sorts of merchants hawking their wares. Typically, the entrepreneur was standing in the bow of the decrepit little rowboat while the "motive power" manned the stern with a long sculling oar. The arrival of these folks was so rapid that I assumed they knew our secret movement orders before we did.

As the vendor climbed the Jacob's Ladder with his arms full, I marveled at his dexterity and balance. Much bowing and scraping with broad smiles followed. The products on offer varied from Noritake china to custom-made suits and shoes. Most likely no vetting process existed to screen these individuals, but I never heard that any of our sailors were cheated.

One ongoing problem, however, was that the custom-made and artfully fitted kangaroo-hide Wellington boots, while looking stylish and feeling comfortable, squeaked noisily when you walked. This was embarrassing and annoying. And then, suddenly on one trip a solution appeared: No-Squeak Lee! What a welcome presence – his business boomed. I was measured, had my first trial fitting, and the next day took possession of my beautiful new kangaroo-hide Wellington boots! I loved them and wore them daily, but sadly kangaroo hide is not as tough as cowhide.

Various other services were supplied to sailors in far-off Asia. The employment of "comfort women" was an ancient ritual that had been developed into nearly an art form, one that was eagerly enjoyed by some of our sailors. In fact, any ship's personnel returning to the ship after spending the night ashore was required to take a dose of oral antibiotics before leaving the quarterdeck and entering the vessel. These antibiotics, affectionately known as "after-diddle mints," essentially eliminated venereal disease on the ship.

Along this line, another affliction bears mentioning. Occasionally a quietly seated person would suddenly twitch, grimace, jerk a little, and then quietly resume his activity. This was a sure sign of another unwelcome visitor – body lice, also known fondly as "crotch pheasants." Eliminating lice was much more difficult than acquiring them. A wash named Quell was the primary treatment, followed by the tedious process of removing the egg cases – nits – from the individual hair follicles. Fine-toothed combs worked to some extent, but eventually the only sure way to eradicate the little monsters was manual inspection and manual nit picking. I have often wondered how many individuals described as "nit pickers" actually know the origin of the term.

Overall, our visits to Hong Kong were supreme. I acquired my Wellington boots, a Harris tweed sport coat with leather buttons, and a beautiful chalk-stripe three-piece gray suit, all created to order. But time marches on. The boots wore out, I outgrew the jacket, and by the time I was ready to wear the three-piece suit, the only other wearers worked for Al Capone's successor or were in jail.

My Hong Kong visits were such a success that fifty years later I revisited it with my wife and enjoyed it all over again.

CHRISTMAS TREE

We had just moved into our new home, a 1740 Colonial farmhouse. It was Christmastime, so all of us were busy and weary, but we did need a tree. It just seemed like one more burdensome task. Then, looking out the window toward the old pasture, the solution appeared. Standing there like dark sentinels in the snowy field were scattered evergreen trees. They seemed like a reasonable solution.

All bundled up, we fetched the saw and trudged off to gather the final element of our holiday preparations. Choosing the ideal tree was time-consuming, as we had to weigh all the considerations. Our ceilings were quite low, which was a definite restriction, plus the tree couldn't be too broad due to our large, open fireplaces. Finally, after lengthy cogitation and discussion, the perfect tree was chosen. It was duly felled, and we began to tug it home.

The first part of our chore had been accomplished. Now the sun – and a chill – were descending. We all zipped up our jackets to block a cutting breeze. I pulled down my cap's earflaps.

Dispensing with the fancy protective wraps, old sheets, and tie bands that we had planned to use on the tree, we unceremoniously dragged it home. The tree stand had been set up in a carefully chosen spot and its tray filled with water, all fixed securely. Enough for today, we'll decorate it tomorrow!

The next day an odd aroma permeated the entire living room, most especially pronounced in the far corner where our new little friend, "Christmas Tree," resided. As the day progressed, the strange, unpleasant odor became more and more disagreeable. It reminded us of strong cat urine, but our cat would have none of it and promptly disappeared upstairs. Even our dog, a docile English Setter – but one with a most sensitive nose – opted out of our little party.

Now we started to notice an itchy rash on our hands and arms where we had touched this infernal piece of vegetation. It was then that we looked much more carefully at our tree and realized we had selected a red cedar tree, not a pine tree. Being sensible people, we went to visit a neighbor who had a Christmas tree farm, bought the correct tree, and resumed our festive preparations.

The moral of this story, as we learned, is that not all evergreen trees are created equal.

THE PIGS

Life in a semi-rural area can sometimes become boring, and when it becomes boring for little boys, bad things can happen. To dodge that outcome, one way was to join a 4-H Club.

Our 4-H Club was supervised by an older girl who lived on a pig farm a few miles away. For one project, not surprisingly, we decided to raise and train two white Hampshire piglets supplied by a program at the University of Connecticut. It was February and still bitterly cold in Connecticut, so suitable housing was necessary – an empty box stall in the back of the barn was decided upon. Fresh clean straw was spread, and a heat lamp rigged up to provide safe warmth for "Sue" and "Wee." Keeping the pigs in their own bedroom had been requested, but that idea was swiftly and firmly vetoed by the commander-in-chief.

The first thing I noticed was how fastidious

the little pigs were. Even at the early age of eight weeks they avoided depositing waste near their food or bedding. The piglets seemed to eat incessantly!

Even to this day I don't understand why arsenic is a vital component of the porcine diet. What I did understand back then was that we needed to find a reliable source of extra food to supplement the commercial feed. Here's where my friend Ronnie Wade came to the rescue. He farmed multiple fields in the area and had a roadside vegetable market at the end of our road, about a mile away. Fortunately for us, at Ronnie's market a large amount of surplus greenery was always available, such as damaged ears of corn, outer leaves of lettuce heads, and spoiled melons. The piglets loved the melons, but if the fruit was at all salvageable they had to share it with the rest of us.

To care for the piglets, I established a routine. I would stop at Ronnie's market on the way home if I could get away on time, pick up a large cardboard box crammed with all sorts of produce saved by Ronnie, put the box in the trunk of my car, and head for home and the squealing piglets. They were always so glad to see me – it was really gratifying. When warmer weather arrived, we built them a new pen with a little house under a big pine tree. Again, they adapted so well and so quickly it was remarkable.

After several months of this routine, I became aware of strange looks from some of the other customers at the vegetable stand. I mentioned it to Ronnie, who replied, "You were just too busy carrying garbage to notice."

I should mention that a year or so previously I had received, as partial payment of a bill, a 1956 Bentley sedan that was a bit aged but in great shape. I drove this car daily, so it was quite usual for me to appear at Ronnie's vegetable store on my way home. The only unusual thing, from the perspective of the customers at Ronnie's market, was the loading of a large box of cast-off vegetables and fruit into the trunk of my handsome car. I babied that car, even fixing up a parking place in the barn for it, complete with special lighting, carpeting, and drive-on ramps for servicing it myself.

All went well until one busy Friday evening, when Ronnie's lot was jammed full of neighbors grabbing food for the weekend. For the first time, my beloved car refused to start. It seems this model had a design flaw, a possible dead spot in the starter mechanism. From what I had previously read in the manual, I needed to put the car in gear and rock it back and forth until the dead spot was passed. This required the immediate enlistment of several other people, including Ronnie. We pushed and rocked and wiggled the car, and although I didn't hear any jeers from the bystanders, hushed muttering was obvious. Luckily, when I got into the car it started right up. After thanking Ronnie for his assistance, I continued home. Whatever the problem was, it never occurred again in all the years I drove that car. I'm told that Bentleys have a mind of their own. Mine certainly did.

Oh, by the way, at the end of the summer at the 4-H Club fair, son Hazen won first place for pig showmanship and second place for market hog. Another interesting summer project!

THE FALL OF MARY

Mary got out of bed on a Monday night while Bill was watching television in the den. He heard her cry out, "Oh God!" and then crash down the stairs into the front door of the house. He saw her at the foot of the stairs, and said, "Mary, pull yourself together and then I'll try to help you up and get you back upstairs." When there was no response of any kind, he attempted to move her, realized she was seriously injured, and called 911 for help.

After lengthy evaluation in the hospital, Bill was told that she had sustained a massive stroke followed by the fall down the stairs that had caused a severe skull fracture with traumatic brain damage. There was no hope. The doctors said that after the family had a chance to confer, and to visit Mary, the decision could be made to discontinue all artificial life-support measures.

A meticulous engineer by training and nature, Bill immediately proceeded with funeral arrangements for Saturday. Old Father Gengras agreed to conduct the service for his longtime friends who had helped recruit him many years earlier.

By Wednesday the family had gathered. Even Mary's sister, Patsy, appeared. Only Bill and Mary's son, Greg, lived locally. After a few moments of silence and meditation, the external support systems were turned off. The doctor informed the family that all bodily functions would cease in an hour or so. Time slipped by. One hour ... two hours ... three hours ... and nothing changed. After six hours, mild panic settled over the group, which was much smaller now. The memorial service was already scheduled for Saturday. The reception food had been ordered, and a room for a buffet luncheon had been reserved. Even the cremation, made necessary by lack of room in the family plot, had been reserved. All these unexpected complications whirled through Bill's well-ordered mind. At seven hours, when the situation still hadn't changed, Patsy was heard to mutter, "Mary, you never were on time!" Finally, it all ended, peacefully and quietly.

Saturday came, and as the time drew near to leave for the memorial service, an hour-and-a-half drive, I became more and more disinclined to go. Fate seemed to collaborate with my reluctance – my pants were too tight; I couldn't find matching socks; my dress shoes hurt my feet that had been unshod for two months; and the quintessential disaster – I couldn't find my cufflinks. Ultimately, we did leave Mystic for Hartford – in silence, but we did leave.

At the church entrance, we signed the guest register, received a memorial card, and headed in. Bill, looking haggard and distraught, was darting around like a nervous maître-d'. He shook our hands, patted me on the back, grasped my arm, and thanked us profusely for coming. He said he had meant to call us but couldn't remember whether he had – actually he had called twice.

He then turned his attention to a pair of elderly women just ahead of us. "Never felt a thing," he said to them. "She had no pain. She had a massive stroke and fell down the stairs. Hit her head on the front door. Blood all over the place – out her nose, out her ears, out her mouth. Not a pretty sight, not a pretty sight."

Now the ladies were walking considerably slower, wobbling slightly, as Bill continued with more details. "Yeah, no pain, never felt a thing," he said. "The doctors said it was all over, so we pulled the plug."

The ladies slowed even more, looking much paler. Even I was beginning to feel a little queasy.

The music started, so we sat down. After a moving homily we lined up for a reception in the parish hall, where kind, elderly nuns supervised the buffet luncheon. I was an immediate convert.

And then there was Greg. Bill and Greg had never really been on good terms. Multiple crises had concluded with Bill depositing all Greg's belongings on the back porch and locking all the doors of the house.

Nonetheless, Greg greeted us enthusiastically, chattering away. "You're doing it right, moving to a smaller house," he said. "Mom and Dad's place was too big, too much for them. They should have moved out a long time ago."

Then Greg went on and on about fixing the well at his new place, which he shared with his significant other, as well as describing several other projects that had nothing to do with his mother."

He continued, "You knew my mother had poor balance for years."

Yes, that was true. We knew she had had hypertension and a stroke early on, probably in her thirties. Most recently, we had noted her difficulty getting out of Bill's tiny sports car in our driveway. Finally, she had struggled out of the car, clutched the roof, paused, then slowly and unsteadily walked to our door.

"You know her feet were too small for her body," Greg said. "She was top-heavy, too big in the top half and very small feet. She always said that was a problem for her."

Greg expanded on this unusual explanation for his mother's demise while I tried to change the subject and return to eating lunch. Finally, it was time to leave.

"Greg, nice to see you again and thank you for your hospitality," I said.

"Yeah, thanks for coming," Greg said. "You know how upset my father is. I don't want him to lose it completely, so I plan to check in on him daily."

"Well, Greg, that's very thoughtful," I said.

We knew full well that considering Bill and Greg's strained relationship, a daily "checking in" by Greg would unquestionably be the most likely factor to cause Bill to "lose it completely"!

It was time to go. Goodbyes said, out the door, into the car, and home.

I hate funerals!

THE RACCOON

Our phone rang sharply – it was Alice, our neighbor a few miles down the road, asking if we would like a baby raccoon. Their dog had the little creature cornered in a drain in front of their house and they didn't know what to do. Naturally we said yes, and soon they appeared at our door with a shoebox containing old rags and a tiny animal with its eyes barely open.

Barbara assumed the duties of a substitute mother. An eyedropper was found, cleaned, and filled with warm milk. The center of attention, now dubbed Ralph, grasped the dropper with both forepaws and demonstrated a healthy understanding of how to feed.

Our son George, age seven or eight, was fascinated with Ralph and took on more and more of the responsibilities. Soon they were inseparable. Everywhere George went, Ralph went too.

We made sure that Ralph received all the necessary shots but neglected to have him neutered. Our mistake was brought home when we spotted Ralph on the stone wall behind the kitchen making amorous moves on Smokey, a neutered male cat who appeared totally uninterested.

George's passion for fishing was satisfied by several nearby farm ponds with enough sunfish, catfish, and crappies to keep him entertained for hours. He was always accompanied by Ralph, who rode on George's shoulder or the bike's handlebars. One day a neighbor pulled over in her car and shouted, "Is that a raccoon?!" Before George could answer – SNAP! – another mailbox toppled over, a victim of the neighbor's big white Cadillac! One day a news photographer even stopped to take pictures. Ralph was busy finding and eating tadpoles and looked up only briefly.

Things changed on the day that John, George's older brother, was letting Ralph eat ice cream off his fingertip. Ralph was delighted but was unable to distinguish between the ice cream and the finger and refused to let go. We decided it was time for Ralph to move on. We dropped him off at a distant state park but when we finally got home there was Ralph sitting at the kitchen door – he got home before we did!

Our relationship was now strained. The final time we allowed Ralph in the house the heavy screen door shut on his tail, giving it a distinctive kink.

Winter came, and everything returned to normal. We thought the Ralph problem had been solved. Then one night we saw a raccoon foraging through spilled garbage bags. It had a very distinctive kink in its tail. Yep, it was Ralph. He looked big, fat, and healthy. We raccoon-proofed the garbage and Ralph returned to the woods, never to be seen again.

OVERSEAS ADVENTURE 1

It was Tuesday, October 5, 1999, and we were excited to begin our journey to Europe to visit our longtime friends, the Roberts, who lived on Guernsey, one of the Channel Islands. With our belongings loaded in the car, we headed for the airport in Providence, Rhode Island.

On arriving at our Continental Airlines departure gate at 3 p.m., we noticed that another plane scheduled to depart at 1:30 p.m. was still at hand, now scheduled to leave some hours later. Hoping this was not an omen of things to come, we settled down to pass the time by reading. Fortunately, our flight took off right on time, heading to London via Newark, New Jersey.

At the Newark airport, the gate noted on our boarding pass was teeming with scores of Hasidic Jews clad in long, black coats and flat, wide-brimmed black hats covering long, curled hair. Again, we sensed a possible mix-up. On checking with the airline, we learned that our flight had been moved to another boarding area. We departed for London roughly on time.

Flashing a winsome smile, a flight attendant gave us hot towels to wash our hands and placed cups of water on our tray tables. Dinner followed, then tedium and fatigue. I read *Newsweek* from cover to cover, then tried to rest. Sleep was difficult because my head jutted above the short seatback. In desperation I put my pillow and folded blanket on the tray table and tried to lower my head onto that bundle. A fine idea, but the space was so small that I couldn't get my head all the way down. Needless to say, I had very little rest.

The only excitement on this leg of the journey was the loss of Barbara's eyeglasses. They had fallen somewhere, but the seats were so tightly packed together that I couldn't reach down to feel around for them. We finally enlisted the help of a flight attendant, a pleasant, tanned woman who used her flashlight to discover Barbara's glasses lodged between the seats. A disaster averted! Can you imagine an entire week of having to read French menus to a wife fluent in French, when I had passed my language requirement in Latin and Greek?

We finally arrived at the Gatwick airport just after dawn and proceeded through a mind-numbing maze of security, passports, and customs before finally presenting ourselves at the Jersey-European Airlines passenger desk. We checked in, and then waited, and waited some more for our continuing flight to Guernsey.

The flight was pleasant – brief and uneventful. We gazed down on Guernsey, a beautiful island gem bathed in a dark blue sea. Interestingly, it was the only part of the British Isles occupied by Germany in World War II.

Mel met us, and we drove a short distance to his home – Waterloo House – a traditional three-story English urban home of white-painted brick, a few hundred years old but in perfect condition.

We dropped our gear on the ground floor, which consisted of a parlor, dining room, and kitchen. Behind the house was a charming walled garden, most definitely not to be called a "backyard."

The most remarkable features were palm trees, large aromatic roses, and the biggest gerbera daisies I had ever seen.

Following lunch, Barbara disappeared upstairs to take a shower to recover from our trying journey. Once finished, she stepped out of the shower only to peer directly into the eyes of Mr. Taylor, the window washer, perched on his two-story ladder. Barbara walked to the window, met his astonished gaze with a calm smile, and drew the blinds.

I have heard that Mr. Taylor has asked to return more frequently.

OVERSEAS ADVENTURE 2

We all took naps after lunch and arose refreshed, ready for Manhattan cocktails and then dinner, a tender, flavorful pork roast Marianne had stuffed with prunes and apricots.

Mel later tried to turn from the local TV station to his satellite service so we could view Stateside programming, but the electrical circuits kept blowing out each time for unknown reasons. Each time this happened, Marianne had to trot downstairs in the dark and reestablish power. This routine became tiresome, so we all went to bed. The Brits still have a bit to learn about modern utilities.

The next day after breakfast we toured the island, which is amazingly semitropical. One of Guernsey's main products is flowers! Apparently the warm currents in the surrounding sea significantly modify the island's climate.

Guernsey's primary metropolis, St. Peter Port,

is basically unchanged over the years – the streets are narrow cobblestone, the buildings local granite.

We stopped for lunch at a restaurant atop the bluffs with a picturesque view of the next island, Sark. The lobstermen pulling their traps in the bay far below looked just like a scene out of New England. Then out of nowhere appeared *Condor*, the catamaran that runs from the Channel Islands to the walled city of Saint-Malo in France. The boat made a rather splashy entry into the small harbor of St. Peter Port and proceeded to discharge all sorts of people and cargo.

Returning to our pursuit of lunch, we found that the main dining room was occupied by members of the local Rotary Club or some such similar group. We ended up seated in a somewhat less elegant section – Mel remained inconsolable about that situation, even after we assured him that no matter where we were seated, the food would be just as tasty.

We indulged in very spicy Bloody Marys that would do justice to a Cajun cookout, causing beads of sweat to break out on my forehead – a surefire method of intake control! Fish and chips and fresh green peas rounded out our meal. It was a delightful experience with a magnificent view to boot.

After returning home, Mel and I decided to walk into town to exchange money in preparation for visiting France the next day. The trip was a breeze, all downhill, but the return was an entirely different matter. Halfway up the hill we stopped to rest on a bench in Candie Gardens. Here I gathered a few acorns from massive white oak trees to plant at home. None of them sprouted – pure Anglican malice!

That evening Mel started a warming blaze in the fireplace grate to counter a chill in the air from clouds and a light drizzle outside. Every room had a similar grate, burning a type of "home coal" – a substance somewhat between traditional hard coal and what we know as soft coal. The cozy warmth was enjoyable but also soporific.

After Mel connected to Dish TV we discovered to our delight that "our team," the New York Mets, were in the playoffs, tied one-to-one. However, Morpheus triumphed over baseball and I never did learn who won.

OVERSEAS ADVENTURE 3

After an enjoyable breakfast in Guernsey with our friends, we headed to the local airport for the short flight to Saint-Malo, France. Instead of a central aisle, the small jet had doors on both the right and left sides for easy access – more like a British railcar than a typical U.S. aircraft. It was a glorious day and the display of blue water and fields of flowers below us was truly beautiful.

On arrival we proceeded a short way to our hotel, checked in, and got organized. After a leisurely saunter along the top of the old wall surrounding the city it was time to think about dinner. The hotel did not have a formal bar, so we drank whatever brown alcoholic beverage was available. A fish dinner seemed appropriate – we were at the seashore, after all – it's too bad the fish had apparently been in Saint-Malo considerably longer than we had!

The following day we continued sightseeing.

Since the sky was growing gloomy and foul weather was predicted, we decided to take the high-speed ferry to Guernsey rather than the little jet. Back on the island, we had a pleasant walk from the dock up the hill to the house.

The next day we left for home, with our itinerary to include stops at three airports – Gatwick near London, LaGuardia in New York, and T.F. Green in Providence, Rhode Island – to be followed by a drive to our home in Mystic, Connecticut.

All went well until we reached New York, where we were supposed to catch our connecting flight to Providence in an hour or so. Instead, we were ushered into an area outfitted with multiple chairs and told to wait. Time passed. Our questions to the airline staff were met with shrugs. Eventually it turned out that we had missed our connection to Rhode Island. The airline staff didn't seem to care that we had expected to board the plane to Providence in the early afternoon, get our car upon arrival, and be home in time for dinner.

As boarding finally began at 7 p.m., the airline staff suddenly realized the flight had been overbooked. If we had learned of this development earlier, we could have rented a car and been home in a couple of hours!

The haggling over which passengers would be bumped from the flight went on for what seemed like forever, but finally we boarded the plane and the plane was fully loaded. Not so fast – *overloaded!* To reduce the plane's weight, we needed to get rid of either some fuel or more passengers. So, we sat there and continued to stew – at least we were on the plane, but by then it was 8:30 p.m. and all of us were hungry and grouchy.

Finally, a fuel truck pulled up, inserted a large hose into a wing, and siphoned out enough fuel that the airline staff felt we could safely take off for Providence. We arrived there at 2 a.m., picked up our car, and were home in bed – worn out, hungry, and exasperated – by 4 a.m.

That memorable but unpleasant experience was eight or ten years ago, and needless to say I have not been near an airplane since – been there, seen that, done that, thank you!

MAKO SHARK

The long-awaited weekend was here. Get out of town or get harassed. A boat named *Friday* was our appropriately named destination at the marina in Saybrook.

Heavily laden with clothing, gear, grub, and more, we waddled down the dock and climbed aboard the boat, a fifty-foot Bertram sport fisherman model. My son, George, joined us and we devised our fish-catching strategy. According to nautical reports, a significant thermal was present off the Atlantis Canyon region of the Atlantic Ocean, indicating the potential for a good day of fishing.

We got underway at 4:30 a.m. The distance was plotted at 110 miles and we cruised at about twenty-seven knots. Our engine burned sixty gallons of diesel an hour, so with 1,100 gallons of fuel on board all was well. Out of the river, through the Race, and past Barbara's old hometown, Montauk, we were soon well on our way.

As we neared our designated area we fitted our fishing lines with large lures designed to mesmerize our quarry. Five lines were trolled, forming an inverted "W" formation behind the slowly moving boat. I don't think there is anything more boring than meandering about the empty ocean, wallowing in the swells. If a fish strikes, of course, it all changes suddenly and dramatically.

The weather report predicted a clear, warm day, and initially this was true. However, as morning became afternoon, the sky slowly dimmed, the wind picked up, and the water grew darker. What had been a gentle rocking motion turned into a steady buffeting by waves of four to six feet. The weather radio was now forecasting not clear skies, but a rapidly deteriorating condition with wind, rain, thunder, and lightning – not an enviable position for us. We decided to call it a day and head home as rapidly as possible. We had pulled in four of our five lines, when suddenly we heard a loud pop followed by the scream of a reel.

"Fish on, fish on!" we all shouted, as though

it was necessary. George jumped back in the chair and started applying pressure on the fish. The wind was strengthening and it was difficult just to stand up, even if we were holding onto something. Finally, the fish could be seen in the curl of an immense wave behind us. It was a massive mako shark.

The plan was to back down into the oncoming waves and scoop the fish into the cockpit. Our first two attempts failed to do anything except flood the cockpit, but on the third try George opened the transom door and we brought the fish onboard. Now an unexpected problem arose – a large, very live shark was thrashing about inside the boat.

Ultimately everything quieted down except the weather, which was growing unpleasant. The seas were treacherous. After several hours of pure misery, we entered Long Island Sound and it was as though someone had just changed the scenery on a stage. The wind and water became calm and the sun came out.

We made our way to the service dock for fuel and to offload our only catch. It was then we discovered that the business part of the dock was occupied by a lone sailboat! What thoughtlessness! We needed fuel and wanted to get rid of the fish. Attempts to stir up or find the owners of the sailboat were unsuccessful.

The dock master suggested, "Why don't you try to back into the side of the dock and tie up at a right angle?"

It sounded simple – except for the wind, the currents, and the fact that that's just not the way a boat is supposed to be secured. At any rate, after considerable jockeying, backing, and filling, we were secured enough to run an elongated fuel line to the diesel tank and were able to manipulate the boom of the weighing scale.

As we did this, the fish slowly came off the cockpit deck and up the side, but when it cleared the side of the boat it swung wildly back to the neutral position, which unfortunately took it right over the sailboat. Their beautiful, polished deck, embroidered cushions, and custom upholstery were now covered in fish blood and slime.

We took on 900 gallons of fuel, sold the iced-down fish to a Japanese buyer who noted its weight as 395 pounds, and made our way back to Saybrook.

FIRST SOLO

My exposure to "flying" was almost totally restricted to commercial business flights. When I arrived in Memphis, Tennessee, for my orthopedic residency, I discovered that one of the other residents had his own little Cessna. It wasn't long before we and our wives had made several pleasant trips together. I was bitten!

We subsequently entered practice in Hartford, Connecticut. After a few years, we moved to Bloomfield, a town more north and east of Hartford, but closer to Bradley Airport. Now the flying bug-bite got serious.

After about 15 or 20 years in practice, life had gotten more organized and I vowed to give flying a try. There was a fine flying school and all sorts of accommodations for lessons, ground school, etc. The school was at night (very schedulable) and flying could be booked on a weekend morning. So off we went.

Naturally all of the early lessons were booked with a certified instructor sitting in the right front seat. He was an Air Force veteran with many hours flying, but most of all, he was very patient and tolerant, and he had an outstanding sense of humor! He would communicate with the tower, take off, get us airborne, and then the training started. I got to take off and he sat and watched, criticized, and corrected.

After many months, and after I completed ground school, he became quite flattering and complimentary. This time he got in the plane and did absolutely nothing but put on the headphones. "Go ahead," he said.

Nervously, I did the pre-flight check, all the other checks and got inside. "OK," he said, "let's go." After taxiing into position according to the instructions of the "tower," we stopped, looked, and when told, proceeded onto the interstate-sized runway, pushed the throttle full-on, sat back ... and you know what? We were very happily in the air.

Being "in the air," even if you're not completely alone is a definitely inspiring sensation. After doing a series of exercises and flying "off to the moon," we ended the session and returned to our original field.

When I got home, Barbara said I was absolutely euphoric. "No," I said. It's just one of the most satisfying feelings and sensations cruising around in the unique beauty and quiet of the sky.

The schooling went on and on. The schedule was interrupted by on-call days in the emergency room or sometimes a family gathering.

Then, all of sudden (to me, at least), the instructor stepped out, walked toward the office and said, "OK, go for it."

"Oh, my God!" was all I could say to myself... there was no one else around at 8 o'clock this bright Sunday morning.

SOLO!

Well, here goes. I did the checks, started the engine and sat watching the prop turning lazily in front of me. Do I really need to do this? I've got a nice home a good practice, three great kids and a wife that really likes me. So – go for it!

Up I went – perfect takeoff (easy). I did all sorts of required maneuvers and then just flew up and up and up. What exhilaration, what peace, what time is it?

I returned toward the still practically deserted field, quiet on this early Sunday. I did the checks, talked with the tower and planned my first solo landing. I followed the tower's instructions, slowly descended and gently touched the runway with just a little bounce, I thought. I taxied to the side. There was the instructor.

"Nicely done," he said. I was ecstatic.

"And the landing was magnificent," he said with a faint smile and a twinkle in his eye – "all six times." Oh well, I do enjoy the practicing.

EBONY

Five days down, five days back. Perfect! Ten chapters to edit and ten days to do it. The United Fruit Company had its banana distribution center in Albany, New York, with freighters shuttling back and forth to its plantation in Honduras. For $330 each, Barbara and I could go in style and enjoy an environment conducive to my work.

Arrangements were made, tickets and passports were acquired, and off we went to Albany. It was a gorgeous spring day. We met the ship's skipper, a Dane who lived in Warwick, Rhode Island. Our quarters were immense, extending almost completely across the ship, with a wide spread of windows providing a panoramic view forward. Only one other passenger was onboard, so we had the run of the ship.

After dinner we got underway. It was the

first time I had ever passed UNDER the George Washington Bridge. We cruised down the river through New York City – the city sparkling in the dark – then out to sea.

As we relaxed in the comfortable lounge adjacent to our stateroom, second mate Werner Seebeck, from Spaden, Germany, joined us, along with his beloved "squeeze box." Music and singing went well into the night. Finally, we turned in and slept soundly to the droning of the ship's engines and the gentle roll of the ocean.

Awakened the next morning by one of the mess boys, we ate a hearty breakfast, set up some deck chairs, and I began work on chapter one. My editing and rewriting went smoothly because each chapter author had been chosen for his experience with a specific facet of spine deformity – poliomyelitis, cerebral palsy, birth defects, trauma, and so on – and for previously expressing his views on appropriate approaches. The goal was to find common ground and develop a methodical approach to treatment. Oddly enough, it was usually the "old pros" who required the most coaxing and constant reminders about deadlines, timelines, and space limitations.

On the fifth day we spent some time walking around Tela, Honduras. Then back on board, where all was ready, so we set off for home. A change of itinerary was announced – we had been warned that this could happen. Our next stop would be Baltimore, Maryland, not Albany. At least it wasn't Bangkok! No problem.

In Baltimore, Werner took us to the train station in the company truck. We boarded a train to Philadelphia where my folks lived. They were surprised – but glad – to see us and the next day put us on a plane to Albany. Our old Bentley was waiting for us, looking dirty in the unpaved lot. By the end of the day, and after a car wash, we were home in Connecticut.

Unexpectedly, we received a message from Werner saying he would like to visit us soon. "Soon" was in about four days and his visit was to last and last, even including a camping trip with the kids and Joko the donkey, but not me.

Finally, friend Werner departed for Germany and life slowly returned to normal. Revenge was sweet – all of us spent a month or so with Werner in Germany. After his time off, he had been promoted to first mate on another ship that went back and forth from Bremerhaven, Germany, to Cameroon in Central Africa. Much of their cargo was rare and fancy wood. That was the last I heard from him for a long time, a year or so. It turned out later that he had made no trips to the United States.

He asked if I would like some ebony, knowing I was a hobbyist. Naturally, I leaped at the opportunity. About a year later, he said he was on a fixed route and had given my ebony to a friend on another ship that was more likely to visit the Eastern United States. Time went by. I heard nothing. He then wrote me that he had taken the wood back from his friend and shipped it by Lufthansa Air to Providence, Rhode Island, the nearest facility the airline served.

I started calling around and finally found out that my piece of wood had been impounded at John F. Kennedy International Airport, but no one had seen fit to notify me. After several weeks, I finally got ahold of someone who claimed to be the freight manager, but I had a difficult time understanding his thick Middle Eastern accent. He then claimed that I had threatened him – for what I do not know. I assured him that if I had meant to threaten him, there would be no room for doubt about it.

Ultimately, it turned out that some kinds of ebony are on the U.S. Department of Agriculture's list of banned imports. I phoned the appropriate section of that department and talked with a delightful lawyer. She asked me which species of ebony I was trying to claim. I told her I had no idea, but it was black and very heavy, bare wood about four-by-six inches and thirty-three inches long. She thought for a minute, then came up with a solution – we would call my piece of ebony by a complex Latin name that just happened to be the name of the species allowed into the United States. Soon an envelope containing a twenty-two-page description of ebony laws and an import permit arrived in my office. A couple more calls to Lufthansa and all was set.

Now, almost four months since the saga began, a piece of ebony with my name on it waited for me at the freight station in Rhode Island. We drove there, to be greeted gruffly by another Middle Easterner with a thick accent who wanted to know why he should not drill multiple holes in this piece of wood. He didn't have a reason, but I suppose one should never let logic stand in the way of official routine.

At long last we departed for home with my treasure intact. It had been a serious trial over a period of almost four years, costing about $224 in freight fees and requiring multiple phone calls to New York, Washington, and Rhode Island and multiple fax messages. Through it all, I had encountered only one helpful soul – the cheery, law-skirting attorney at the Department of Agriculture. God bless America!

PHYSICAL THERAPY

"our hand grips are too low."

So started a one-sided conversation with a local physical therapist. Leaving a friend who I was visiting in the Pavilion, I tried to ignore this freely offered but unsolicited advice until the lengthening silence compelled me to respond.

"Yes, but –" I started to say.

"You should be walking more erect, not all bent over," stated Miss Helpful.

I pondered that. "Yes, I know, but –"

"Here, I'll raise the handles for you – it's so easy."

With that, she raised my grips.

"There, that should get you out of that ugly crouch," she said. "This will improve your upright posture as well as your ability to see in front of you. Now let's see you use the adjusted walker."

I tried to clarify my situation for her, but to no

avail. She continued her rapid-fire spiel.

"Here, try this now," she said. "You'll be so much better."

I muttered, "Don't I wish!" However, somewhat grateful for the attention, I gave up trying to explain. I grabbed the new, higher walker, stood erect as a military cadet, and as I expected, pitched over backward. I watched the ceiling lights zoom overhead, then the fire sprinkler nozzles, then the drapes, then Thunk! Fortunately, I landed on the bed with no harm to anything but my pride.

"What on earth happened?" she exclaimed.

Rapidly I regained my orientation, sat up, and stated in measured words: "I tried repeatedly, but ineffectively, to tell you that if I stand up straight I lose my balance and fall over backward. Thanks for your help. Now if you will please readjust my grips, I'll be on my way."

BAD TIMING

As I passed through the resident activity center – the visceral heart of our small community – I recalled my experiences of last spring almost as vividly as when they occurred.

At Christmastime my son had sent me a handsome Timex watch that displayed not only hours and minutes but also the date, day of the week, and other wondrous features. Best of all, it sported a Velcro wristband, which I cherished above all else because a similar band on my old watch had worn out after many years of use; at that time the local jeweler told me that Velcro watchbands were no longer available. Thus, my delight with the surprise gift of a new watch with my favored band.

Unfortunately, the instructions on the enclosed tissue-paper sheet were so small I could not read them, even with the help of a magnifying glass. Hence, my failing vision was unable to master the new watch.

The impetus for all this busy activity was that blight of human origin known as Daylight Saving Time. What preposterous ghoul ever thought up that horror? But that's another gripe for another day.

Out of desperation I decided to use the services of a representative from a local jewelry company that saw fit to hawk its wares in our common room each Wednesday morning. And so, I arose, gathered up my new watch, and skillfully manipulating my rolling walker, proceeded to seek help in resetting my watch.

There, sitting at an unadorned card table set to one side, was a mature woman accompanied by a small sign denoting the jewelry company's name. She had no customers, so I approached the card table and started to announce myself.

"Oh, you have to sign in first," was the only response I received.

She fumbled around, finally producing a tattered clipboard with a sheet of paper on it, along with a pencil. I signed my name.

By this time, several women who had been

hovering in the area approached the table, signed in, and proceeded to converse with the saleswoman. I went to one side, found a soft seat, and waited my turn again.

Well, women came, and women went, and all of them seemed to be on a first-name basis with the woman at the card table.

Finally, I went over, interrupted their conversation, and said, "Excuse me, but all I want is someone to help me set my new watch because I can't read the instruction sheet." That done, I again sat down.

Then, as if out of nowhere, a voice rang out, "James Hardy!"

I immediately got up, manned my walker, and marched toward the card table.

"May I help you?" she asked flatly.

"Yes, I don't know how to reset this new watch for Daylight Saving Time and I thought someone from your store might help me out."

She glanced at the sparkling Timex in my hand, carefully avoided touching it, and chirped, "Oh, we don't have anything to do with inexpensive items such as that."

A moment of strained silence ensued, following which I muttered a vile but heartfelt curse under my breath.

I returned home, dug out an old watch already set on Daylight Saving Time, and solved my own problem – with a watch for summer and a watch for winter.

Regarding the watch saleswoman, I don't know whether she had any bad experiences after our little interaction, but if so, I would like to believe that I was solely responsible.

CANOE CLUB CANNON

I have no idea where the little cannon came from. I just knew it had always been there, sitting on top of the old upright piano in the back corner of the Canoe Club for as long as I could remember. It was very heavy and measured about a foot wide and a bit longer.

Despite the name, in reality this establishment was a men's luncheon club on the Connecticut River. Maybe in years' past canoes had been involved, and maybe the cannon had some particular relevance to the club, but if so, that was before my time.

One day, for no particular reason, the conversation turned to the little cannon on top of the piano. One person who seemed to be more familiar with the situation than the rest of us claimed it took a 10-gauge shotgun shell. Wow, that's a lot of pop! I had never personally seen a 10-gauge shotgun shell. When deer hunting I had used 12-gauge shells and even those were quite large. When bird hunting we usually used 16-gauge or even 28-gauge shells.

The cannon's purpose was discussed on several additional occasions. Maybe it was used as a starting gun for races. Perhaps it was fired off during celebrations. Possibly it was used to sound a salute, such as for "the Governor of the Fair State of Connecticut."

At any rate, after many unproductive discussions, one individual came up with a clever proposition: "Why don't we try to fire it and see what happens?"

This was a particularly stellar idea, considering that only a few hard-core members would be present on the date chosen for the firing of the cannon.

The individual who seemed to know the most about the cannon was designated "Chief Gunner" and given a badge. Over the next week or so, plans were made, equipment obtained, and most importantly of all, blank 10-gauge shotgun shells were bought.

On the fateful day, the cannon was lugged out to the edge of the front lawn, overlooking the serene Connecticut River. It was a lazy, sunny summer day.

The Chief Gunner had found an old bottle brush that could be used to clean out the barrel, if that ever truly needed to be done. You often saw that kind of thing in old movies, so reason enough. No other adjustments could be made to the cannon – you just pointed it!

All was ready. The shell was loaded, the breech closed and locked, and a long cord was attached so that Chief Gunner could safely shelter behind the clubhouse while performing his duties.

Gunner hollered "Clear!" which is probably more applicable to starting small airplane engines than small cannons, but seemed appropriate at the time.

At that very moment the tourist boat *Lady Fenwick* appeared around the bend. Gunner pulled the cord. A resounding roar was accompanied by a massive cloud of smoke that completely obscured the boat.

We nearly panicked, but all manner of shouts, yells, and curses led us to believe that everyone onboard *Lady Fenwick* was alive and well. As the smoke cleared, we saw that the boat had made a

180-degree turn and was heading downstream, returning to Saybrook much more rapidly than it had come.

It's been a long time since that episode, but the little cannon still sits quietly on top of the old upright piano in the back corner, awaiting its next call to active duty.

THE PILL

Duh ... Duh ... Duh ... DUM!

My hearing aid battery was warning me that it was running low and needed to be replaced. Dutifully, I exchanged the old battery in the right earpiece for a fresh one. I continued to get ready for bed and all seemed well.

The weather had been cool, snotty, and overcast – windy with occasional drizzle – generally unpleasant and not the sort of climate Florida's tourist bureau would voluntarily publicize. Good note, though – no snow.

Nevertheless, the inclement weather certainly had a distinct relationship to my feeling of well-being, or rather the lack thereof. Aches and pains had plagued me all day in my knees, hips, and back.

"Why don't you try an Aleve pill at bedtime tonight?" asked Barbara.

Well, okay, what's to lose?

After washing myself, scrubbing my teeth, putting in my eyedrops, and taking the day's scheduled medications, I turned off the light in the bathroom, grabbed my walker, and proceeded into the living room in pursuit of an Aleve and some water.

There on the coffee table in the dim light was the vague outline of a pill. Down went the pill without a hitch. I thought to myself, how clever of these research pharmacists to make a general-purpose pill with no bitter aftertaste that's so small and smooth that it doesn't stick in the throat but slips right down.

After turning off the lights, crawling into bed, and falling asleep, I had no aches or pains that night. Maybe the pill worked as advertised, or maybe it was just the delightful change in the weather.

Barbara asked if I had tried Aleve after she left the bottle out.

"No, I didn't see the bottle, but I took the pill on the coffee table," I replied cheerily.

Then I realized – or feared – what had happened. Quickly I sorted out the container the spare batteries had come in, to check the warnings and other instructions. "Keep out of the reach of children" – that seems reasonable. "Dispose of properly" – okay, that's a given. Lastly was a warning – "Do not incinerate."

Well, now I realized what had happened. A hearing aid battery sure did look like an Aleve pill in the dark. Who knows, maybe it did help. As far as cautious disposal is concerned, I'll just have to do the best I can.

TREES

In 1991 we lived on the Connecticut shore and divided our time between there and work in the Hartford area. Our son, John, was married and wanted to live in the family house, which we all did, briefly and comfortably. The schizophrenic lifestyle of trying to dwell in two places at the same time finally became too tedious, so we settled permanently in Mystic, Connecticut, like an old snail withdrawing into its shell.

The house was on the water with vistas of Fishers Island, the sound, and the Atlantic Ocean off to the left. This scene was framed by a large old Norway maple tree that dominated the landscape with rich deep-green foliage that became a blazing yellow-orange in the fall. Raking leaves from the tree was only a minor problem because the perpetual wind blew them away.

The weather by the shore seemed to be sharper

than inland, despite local and national meteorologists claiming that the shore temperatures were moderated by the surrounding waters. Maybe so, but statistics don't always translate into actuality.

On one occasion, late in August, "intermittent showers" were predicted, "associated with some scattered lightning strikes" and chilly nighttime temperatures. We had gone to bed and snuggled under the covers feeling safe and secure, awaiting the predicted rainstorm. It would be good for the vegetable garden, I thought.

It was a very dark night. No rain yet, but heat lightning flared in the distance and I heard the ominous rumbling of the impending storm. The wind got spooky – swerving first from the northeast and then quickly shifting to the southeast with increasing gusts that caused our trees by the water to twist and bow like servile minions, a worrying wind that predicted the unpredictable.

Slowly the clatter of rain started. It soon became a downpour, so intense that anything more than fifty feet from the house was totally obscured. Amid the howling wind and the din of the driving rain came the first sudden crash of thunder, accompanied by a blinding flash of lightning. Its viciousness woke me from a sound sleep. Barbara slept on, obviously desensitized by years of late-night phone calls.

Suddenly there was a second, much more dramatic flash, and a crash that shook the house. This blast was so severe that Barbara seemed to bounce a foot or so up off the bed. Now she was definitely awake. And frightened. The wind, rain, and lightning continued. A sharp odor of ozone hung in the air, along with a palpable sensation of static electricity.

Slowly the violence of the storm subsided. The lights went out. All the digital clocks blinked "12:00" thanks to battery backup, but otherwise we were in the dark. There was nothing we could do about it, so we went back to sleep.

In the morning, after resetting all the clocks, we started to assess the damage. First, all the circuit boards in the overhead electric garage doors had been cooked. This meant I had to figure out how to manually operate the doors, so I could leave for work. The television was also cooked. Other electrical devices, such as the circuit breakers, were destroyed, and who knows what other damage we might find.

In the dim light of dawn, we began to survey the damage outside. Looking from the back door toward the water, the devastation was apparent. Brush and debris were scattered about the yard, various bushes were roughed up, tall flowers were knocked over – but the most devastating discovery was that our beautiful Norway maple tree by the stone wall was totally flattened. And I mean flattened – spread around the yard and the other side of the wall as though it had never existed.

The maple tree had been such an integral part of our waterfront vista that we decided to plant a replacement. We selected a pin oak, a more shoreline-tolerant species. That tree has thrived and is now so tall, over fifty feet, that I worry about a repeat episode impacting multiple electrical and digital functions in our home, courtesy of wind, rain, and lighting.

About ten years ago, around the time of the great disaster to the Norway maple tree, we found a seedling of that tree growing wild in my vegetable garden. Subsequently we potted the seedling, nurtured it for a couple years, and eventually transplanted it along the back stone wall. The sapling is now showing great promise for future growth. It may well become our new challenge to the petulant gods of the stormy sky.

"DRAFT" HORSE

I recently read about a young woman who was arrested for "driving under the influence" while traveling down the main street of a town – on horseback! I suppose the situation was settled amicably, or at least I hope so. Can you imagine a fine young lady just trying to ride her horse through town, even if it had only a few stores and no major mall? I never forgot this tale, and never attempted to emulate her experience.

Years later, I was a practicing orthopedist in Connecticut, living in an old 1740 house on an old farm. Over time we amassed quite a collection of animals, including friendly piglets from the University of Connecticut, a burro named Jocko from a friend of a friend, two riding horses to keep the weeds down, and a pair of goats to eat the weeds the horses rejected. That was the basic animal team, although there were additions and subtractions as time passed.

Usually when I got home in the evening I headed up to the pasture to feed and water the animals. There, a substantial wood post and hog-wire fence with sturdy boards along the top was handy to set items on. It was my habit to place my large glass of a refreshing Manhattan cocktail on the broad cap of the fence and then turn away to rinse and fill the water tank and distribute food.

One evening, I went to reclaim my pre-prandial refreshment only to discover that the glass was empty. Even the ice cubes were gone. Astonished, I looked all around me. Nobody else was there, and all the animals appeared innocent. I could find no debris, no leftovers, nothing to give me a clue.

I shrugged and returned to the house for a refill. Rearmed with a fresh new glass of Manhattans, I fed and watered the animals and completed my chores. As I turned to retrieve my drink, I saw King, the big saddle horse, reach into my glass, curl up his long, red tongue like a long, red straw, and rapidly empty my glass, ice and all. I grabbed the slobbery glass away from him. King looked at me and grinned

– or at least stood there stupidly and bared his teeth – then wandered slowly and rather unsteadily toward his box stall in the back of the barn. I wanted to go back to the house, sit down, and cry. This had not been a good day at all.

Just then, Barbara called out, "You can sit down now, dinner is on the table."

The horse eventually was sold to a Presbyterian minister and his family in Waterbury, Connecticut. Incidentally, I never did get paid for the horse, so he deserved his nonalcoholic fate with a family of teetotalers. I never did hear of a horse with delirium tremens!

GEORGE

It was the weekend of the Superbowl football game. I worked late in the office, hoping I could persuade George to come home with me, spend the weekend at the shore where we now lived, and catch the game on TV. I called him at work several times, but the answer was always the same: "No thanks, Dad. I'm just going to stay home." Over the weekend I tried calling him several times, but there was no answer.

The following week I called again and again – still no answer. Becoming concerned, I contacted a couple of his local buddies and asked them to check on George. After they gained access to his apartment with the help of a policeman they found George "asleep" in bed – dead.

The rest is nothing but a hazy memory. He was identified by a policeman he had known. The undertaker pleaded with me and Barbara not to try to view the body because he had obviously been dead for several days.

The funeral was massive – he had so many friends and associates that our little Episcopal church in Mystic overflowed. Afterward, Barbara and I went home, sat in the kitchen, and wept.

A couple of days later, we boarded our Boston Whaler at our dock and journeyed out into Long Island Sound to take the container of ashes to one of George's favorite fishing holes. We stopped, opened the box of ashes, and sprinkled them in the wind. Now it was all over. George was only thirty-one years old.

Note to future ash spreaders: always scatter ashes with the wind at your *back!*

GARDENING

Running late, I got in my car, put it in gear, stepped on the gas, and CRASH! – the awful, mind-numbing sound of metal tearing metal. Obviously, I had inadvertently put the car in forward rather than reverse. Two bicycles belonging to a neighbor had been parked against the garage wall in front of me. Now they were crumpled and grossly deformed. Immediately, several neighborhood oglers appeared from nowhere, softly clucking, casting glances in my direction. I was just happy that none of them had been under or in front of the car. It was due to this incident that the owner of the bicycles and I became acquaintances and ultimately friends.

Sometime later he and I had another interesting encounter. Despite various back problems resulting in multiple surgeries and poor balance, I had persisted in my hobby of vegetable gardening. It was early spring, and despite my balance and ambulation problems I was standing in the center of my garden plot when I suddenly lost balance and fell backward – plop! – into the soft, recently tilled soil.

Anticipating just such a situation, I had planned to drive some stout poles into the ground to grab onto but had not yet gotten around to it. Flat on my back, unable to sit up or even roll over on all fours, I saw nothing to hold onto.

So, there I was, totally frustrated, cursing to myself, and getting more and more thwarted, when who appears on the adjacent walkway? None other than my neighbor – he of the shiny new bicycles – who had a garden plot not 100 yards down the road from me. He waved cheerily from the pavement. I waved back from my recumbent position, forcing a weak grin and trying to act nonchalant, as though I did all my gardening chores this way – lying on my back in the dirt, gazing up at the sky.

I asked how he was enjoying his new bikes. He said he was having a fine time with them. After a few brief exchanges, he smiled, I smiled, and we parted.

Eventually, I was able to push myself over to

the sturdy, low fence that bordered my garden. With that to assist me, I was able to get onto my knees, dust myself off, and ultimately sit on the railing.

To this day, many years later, I'm sure my neighbor wonders what on earth I was doing lying in the middle of my garden plot conversing with passers-by, apparently making dirt angels.

He never asked, I never volunteered.

WHAT TO DO

During World War II, with all our physicians in the military, I developed an ache in my left ear. As the day progressed, the ache got worse, not better. Finally, by late evening the pain was so severe that something had to be done. Mother called the medical phone number for the Naval services in the area and was told to proceed to St. Agnes Hospital on South Broad Street in South Philadelphia. Gas was rationed, and this was a long and unfamiliar journey, but off we went.

Ultimately, we found the hospital, checked into the emergency room, and took a seat. The aroma of antiseptic and other strange chemicals pervaded the air. The stark room had little in the way of furnishings, was dimly lit, but had a fascinating black-and-white checked tile floor – a definite sign of its vintage.

After what seemed an eternity, a young man

in a rumpled white scrub suit – I thought he was wearing pajamas – with a stethoscope draped around his neck looked in my ear. He may have mumbled something to my mother, but I didn't catch it. He put some capsules in a little envelope and said, "Codeine. Dump the stuff out of the capsule into a spoon and take it with water."

That was that. Home we went. I took the medicine. My ear hurt a lot, but I seemed to forget about it due to fatigue and medication. In the morning, I awoke to find a foul smelling, greenish mess on my pillow – my eardrum had ruptured. I don't remember the specifics after that, but I got better. However, I never sensed that I could hear as well with my left ear as I could with my right ear, although hearing tests showed no loss of ability.

Some seventy-five years later, I was ordered by my spouse to investigate hearing aids. After several cursory examinations, I was sold a fine pair of matched aids. I wore them for a year or so, but noticed no benefit, only irritation.

At this juncture, our family physician got involved. Against my better judgment, I was sent to an audiologist, who subjected me to a series of hearing tests. Finally, we all sat down for the results.

"First of all, you basically have no hearing in your left ear," the audiologist said.

I said I realized that – it was one of the reasons I was there. We then moved into a small conference nook, where we sank deeply into overstuffed leather armchairs. I knew I was trapped – there was no way I was getting out of this monster.

The doctor continued to present her findings. "You realize that a unilateral loss of hearing is frequently associated with an acoustic neuroma," she said.

That got my attention, but as she described hearing aids that transmitted from the good side to the bad side, I began to lose interest.

"Of course, surgery is an option," she said, "but your hearing would not return."

I lost even more interest.

"An MRI scan would help in evaluation and diagnosis," she went on, "but with the number of stents and other metal implants already inserted in you, it would be technically impossible." Met by silence, she finally asked, "What are your feelings?"

"Well," I said, "I am eminently satisfied with my place in the universe at this time. I can see no real need to change anything. I'll play the cards I've been dealt, enjoy it, and forget the unknown."

Barbara had sat silently through the entire process. We then drove home.

Sometimes it's good enough just to know what your options are.

THE CIRCLE

I am born – a great relief to my mother, and the seminal event in the life of James Hazen Hardy III. Still, it's a shocking and unfathomable transition from a secure existence of heat, nourishment, and protection into a harsh, noisy, and unfriendly world.

Vision is poor – if it exists at all initially – and gradually evolves into shadowy retinal images that register a big zero in the primordial occipital cortex of my brain.

Totally dependent, all my meals are now lovingly and efficiently provided. I am perpetually sitting propped up or lying down. Sleeping is a major pastime, interrupted by the cold cleansing of my private parts.

I know nothing and control nothing. Time passes, but not much changes in my life, except that my diet now includes more substantial food.

Vision is improving. Objects initially blurred and indistinct are now clearer and identifiable. Following people with my eyes is not only possible but pleasant.

Walking is a challenge interrupted by frequent falls backward into a sitting position – plop! Amused looks are followed by helping hands.

What is so crucial about walking in the erect position? Well, it's one of the main differences between humans and the other great apes, such as gorillas and chimpanzees, who still basically ambulate on all fours. Standing and walking upright permits humans to use their hands, featuring all-important opposable thumbs, for a huge variety of activities. Chimpanzees are intelligent and entertaining, but they can't play the piano.

After learning to walk, voluntary bladder and bowel control is the next benchmark in life.

As in any human activity, a challenge will eventually arise. Walk, and a footrace will take place. Drive an automobile, and a car race will ensue. Ride a horse, and some other horse must be beaten to the barn. It just shows that once an enduring situation is established, there will be physical, social, and emotional progress.

The boredom of routine marks the middle passage of life, punctuated by positive and negative events, but retirement is largely enjoyable. However, something has subtly changed. Over the course of a seven-decade lifespan, my activity level is decreasing.

Ambulating, especially stair climbing, has become a bit of a problem. Walking becomes more difficult, and balance suffers. A slower gait and a less stable stance ultimately require the use of a cane. Next, joint pain and other uncertainties mandate progression from a simple cane to a more stable walker. Ambulation is reduced over several months. Ultimately the walker is parked in the foyer and life becomes more sedentary.

The eyesight that was so acute has dimmed, though bolstered with glasses. Nevertheless, over the years, vision starts to fail, despite medications and mechanics. Lower back pain, leg pain, and weakness slowly progress. Degenerative arthritis has taken its toll.

Activity becomes more and more limited. Unfortunately, age brings dementia, significant memory loss, and gradual loss of vision. We've been here before – long ago.

Wait – stop! Here I am, healthy and happy. No more depressing thoughts. I have things to do and jobs to finish, so out of the way. Life goes on and I'm in it and loving every minute! See you tomorrow!

Acknowledgments

These stories would not have reached print if not for the overwhelming contribution of my wife, Barbara.

About the Author

James H. Hardy is a retired orthopedic surgeon who writes stories and "musings" while enjoying retirement in Florida.

He is the author of *Reflections*, a book featuring a collection of sixty-five stories. It was published in 2016. In 1971, he was editor of the book, *Spinal Deformity in Neurological and Muscular Disorders*.

Born November 6, 1930 in a suburb of Philadelphia, he grew up in that area and graduated high school from The Episcopal Academy in 1948. He attended Harvard University and earned a chemistry degree in 1952. After graduation, he served two years in the U.S. Navy in Korea.

He returned to enter medical school at Columbia College of Physicians and Surgeons in the class of 1958. Upon graduation, he did an internship at St. Luke's Hospital in New York City where he met his future wife, Barbara Hulse. After completion of a two-year stint as a research fellow in orthopedics, he and Barbara moved to Memphis, Tennessee, where he completed a residency in Orthopedic Surgery at the Campbell Clinic.

December 1964 heralded the couple's arrival in Hartford, Connecticut, where he entered the practice of orthopedic surgery.

Since 2003, he has been retired and living in Florida where, in addition to writing, he enjoys reading, vegetable gardening, and making up for lost time with family.

www.ingramcontent.com/pod-product-compliance
Lightning Source LLC
Chambersburg PA
CBHW022216090526
44584CB00012BB/756